Fact Finders®

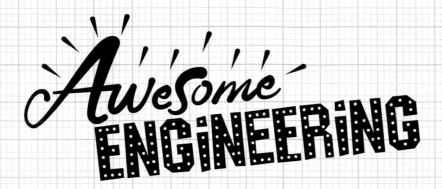

BRIDGES

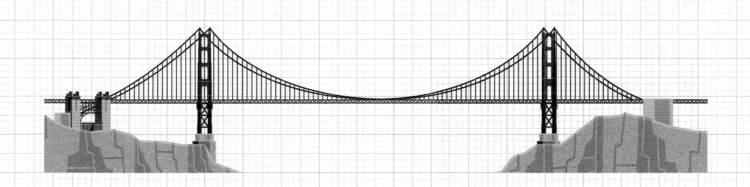

SALLY SPRAY

WITH ARTWORK BY MARK RUFFLE

CAPSTONE PRESS

a capstone imprint

Fact Finders Books are published by Capstone Press,
1710 Roe Crest Drive, North Mankato, Minnesota 56003
www.mycapstone.com

Library of Congress Cataloging-in-Publication Data
Library of Congress Cataloging-in-Publication data is available on the Library of Congress website.

978-1-5435-1334-9 (library binding)
978-1-5435-1340-0 (paperback)

Editorial Credits

Series editor: Paul Rockett
Series design and illustration: Mark Ruffle
www.rufflebrothers.com
Consultant:
Andrew Woodward BEng (Hons) CEng MICE FCIArb

Photo Credits

Leonid Andronov/Shutterstock: 6; Vichaya Kiatying-Angsulee/Alamy: 29cl; Anyaivanova/Shutterstock: 14; unknown photographer for Benjamin Baker/Wikimedia Commons: 11; Andrey Bayda/Shutterstock: 9; Ben Bryant/Shutterstock: 28tr; Cpaulfell/Dreamstime: 19; Dvoevnore/Shutterstock: 13; Mary Evans PL: 10; Olga Gavrilova/Shutterstock: 29cr; Joyfull/Shutterstock: 26; Michal Kniti/Dreamstime: 28tc; Nicola Messana Photos/Shutterstock: 7; R.M.Nunes/Shutterstock: 23; PHB.cz (Richard Semik)/Shutterstock: 24; Terry Reimink/Dreamstime: 29c; seanelliottphotography/Shutterstock: 28tl; Hiroshi Tanaka/Dreamstime: 21; Andrew Zarivny/Shutterstock: 16

First published in Great Britain in 2017
by The Watts Publishing Group
Copyright © The Watts Publishing Group, 2017

TABLE OF CONTENTS

GET OVER IT!

Bridges create connections between places, allowing people to travel and trade. Humans have been building bridges for thousands of years. As building techniques have developed, so have the shapes, the weight bridges can carry, and the lengths they can span.

The Iron Bridge was the first arch bridge to be made from cast iron. It was completed in 1781 and crosses the River Severn in England. Iron is not a strong enough material to be used for long bridges; this bridge is 100 feet long.

*In 1929, the 89-ft-long Maurzyce Bridge in Poland became the world's first completely **welded** bridge. **Steel** welding has allowed **engineers** to build bridges in all shapes and sizes with far greater spans.*

EARLY BRIDGES

One of the earliest surviving bridges is the Arkadiko Bridge in Greece, which was built around the 13th century BC. This small arch bridge is 13 feet high and 72 feet long. It was built from **limestone** rocks packed tightly together and held in place by their weight. Built over a small stream, it let chariots speed along on their journey and even had curbs in place to guide the wheels.

The Romans built the Alcántara Bridge in Spain between AD 104 and 106. The bridge is made of stone and a type of cement, called pozzolana, which is made from volcanic ash.

*The development of steel meant bridges could be made longer and stronger. Gustave Eiffel, **designer** of the Eiffel Tower, built the magnificent Garabit Viaduct in 1895. This arched **truss** bridge spans a large valley and carries trains traveling to and from the south of France.*

*The Anji Bridge in China was finished in AD 605 and is still standing more than 14 centuries later. Designed by Li Chun, the curve is made from limestone fixed with **iron**. When the water rises, it flows through the top arches.*

0   80   160   240   320   400   480   560   640   720   800   880

Length in feet

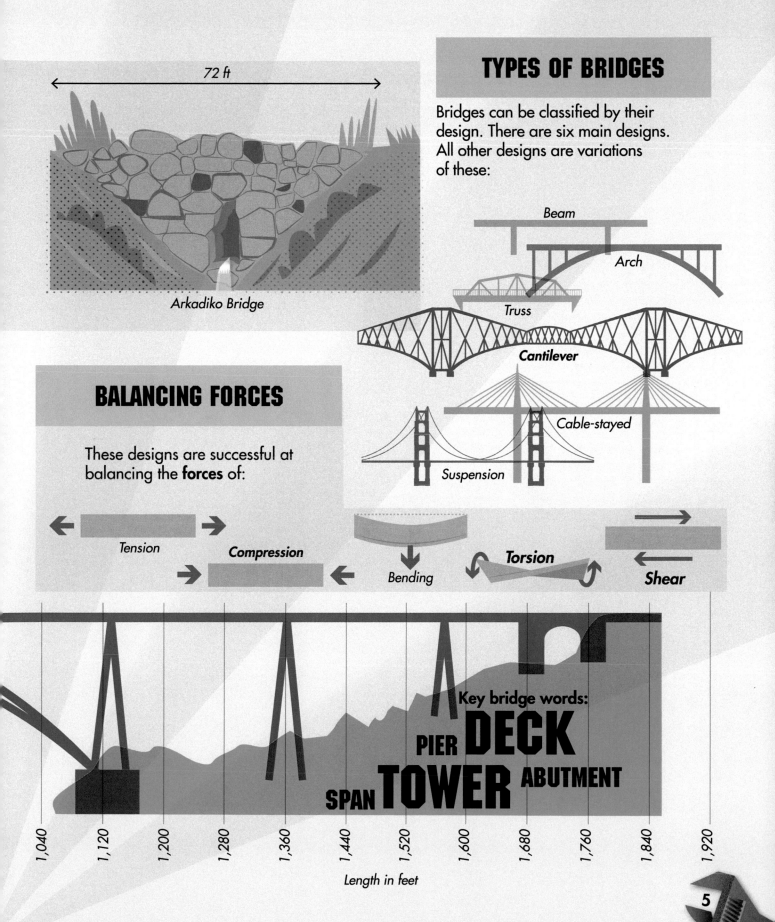

72 ft

Arkadiko Bridge

TYPES OF BRIDGES

Bridges can be classified by their design. There are six main designs. All other designs are variations of these:

Beam

Arch

Truss

Cantilever

Cable-stayed

Suspension

BALANCING FORCES

These designs are successful at balancing the **forces** of:

Tension

Compression

Bending

Torsion

Shear

Key bridge words:

PIER **DECK**

SPAN **TOWER** ABUTMENT

1,040   1,120   1,200   1,280   1,360   1,440   1,520   1,600   1,680   1,760   1,840   1,920

Length in feet

SI-O-SEH POL

Si-o-Seh Pol is a magnificent example of an arch bridge. Built from stone and brick between 1599 and 1602, it stretches across the Zayandeh River in Isfahan, Iran. Its name means "bridge of 33 arches" in the Farsi language, as this is the number of big arches in the design.

There are two tiers of arches along the bridge.

BUILDING BRIEF

Construct a bridge to cross a river and unite the north and south sides of Isfahan.
It should be sturdy enough to withstand the fast river and have high sides to protect pedestrians from strong winds and the sun.

Builder: Ostad Hossein Banna (overseen by Allah Verdi Khan Undiladze)

Location: Isfahan, Iran

WHAT'S SO GOOD ABOUT AN ARCH BRIDGE?

Arch bridges neatly distribute the compression force both through the arch—into the supporting piers—and along the length. The piers are held in place at the ends of the bridge by **abutments**. These stop the arch from spreading out and collapsing.

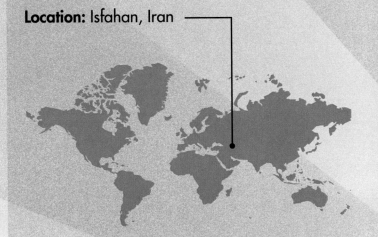

*Si-o-Seh Pol is 977 ft long, with two rows of arches. The arches on the bottom row support the bridge **deck**. The arches above are decorative **parapets** that do not support anything.*

FOUNDATIONS

Bridges must be built on strong **foundations** sunk into the ground. To build the Si-o-Seh Pol, the river was diverted so the foundations could be dug down into the **bedrock**. Its foundations were lined with **earthenware** pipes filled with rubble and mud. This supports the stone piers that in turn support the arches. The abutments were put in place to support each end of the bridge ready for the next stage of the build.

*The deck of the bridge carries the "**live load**" of pedestrians.*

KEYSTONE

The last stone to be put in place is called the keystone. During construction, the bridge's arch has to be supported from underneath. The keystone is like the last piece of a jigsaw puzzle. Once it is put in place, the supports can be taken away and the arch becomes self-supporting.

For every force (action), there is an equal and opposite reaction. So, as the load pushes the keystone downward, the force is distributed down through the arch, and the ground pushes back through the bridge's arch to the keystone. The force also pushes sideways into the abutments, which apply a balancing force and help keep the bridge stable.

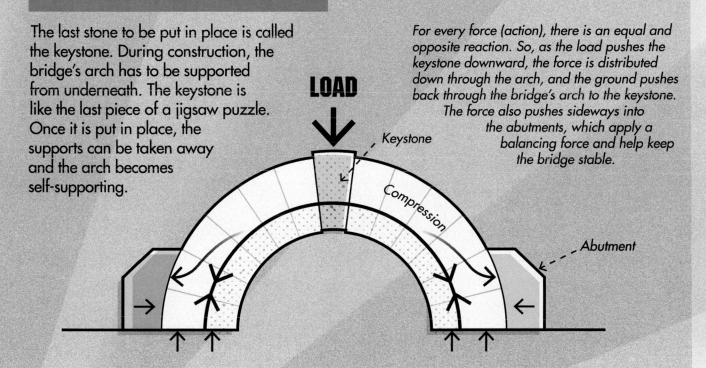

LOAD

Keystone

Compression

Abutment

BROOKLYN BRIDGE

When it was opened in 1883, the Brooklyn Bridge in New York City was the longest suspension bridge in the world. It was a huge project. But it was a dangerous project too—more than 20 construction workers died.

BUILDING BRIEF

Design and build a bridge to cross the East River, linking Manhattan with Brooklyn. It will replace the overused and unreliable ferry service and help businesses survive in Brooklyn.

Engineers: John A. Roebling, Washington Roebling, Emily Roebling

Location: New York City, USA

Length 5,989 ft

CAISSONS

The foundations for the enormous bridge were dug out of the riverbed using devices called **caissons**. Caissons resemble upturned wooden barrels open at the bottom. To sink them to the bottom, the stone towers were built on top, pushing them into the **silt** of the riverbed. Air was pumped in, giving the workers, who were nicknamed "sandhogs," access to dig out the silt. Building of the towers continued on top as the workers dug down to the bedrock. Once the work was complete the air space was filled with stones to complete the construction of the towers.

CABLES

The suspension bridge's huge granite towers stretch 276 ft above the water and support the main steel cables. These are **anchored** at each end of the bridge to stones weighing nearly 60,000 tons. The main cables are made from 5,434 separate steel wires that were spun together on-site. More steel cables attach the bridge deck to the main cables in vertical and diagonal patterns.

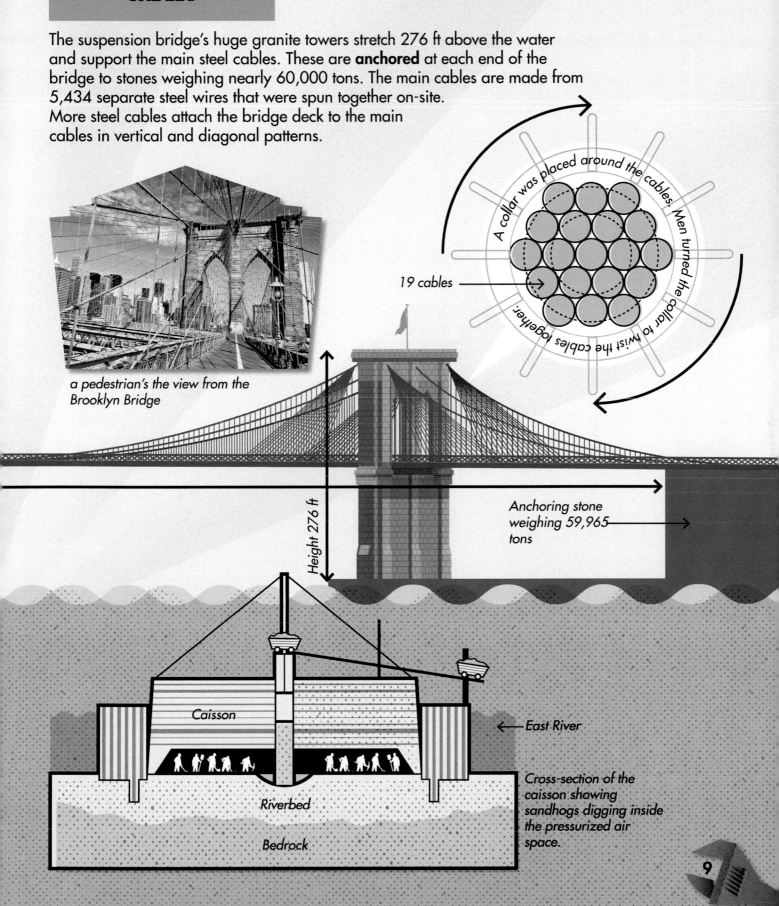

a pedestrian's the view from the Brooklyn Bridge

A collar was placed around the cables. Men turned the collar to twist the cables together.

19 cables

Height 276 ft

Anchoring stone weighing 59,965 tons

Caisson

East River

Riverbed

Bedrock

Cross-section of the caisson showing sandhogs digging inside the pressurized air space.

FORTH BRIDGE

This majestic rail bridge crosses the Firth of Forth in Scotland and carries up to 200 trains per day. It opened in 1890 after nearly a hundred years of planning and eight years of building work.

the Forth Bridge during construction

BUILDING BRIEF

Design a rail bridge to cross the estuary, replacing the ferry links. Take into account the unsupportive riverbed, the high winds, and the heavy loads of freight to be transported safely across.

Engineer: Sir John Fowler

Designer: Sir Benjamin Baker

Location: Firth of Forth, Scotland, UK

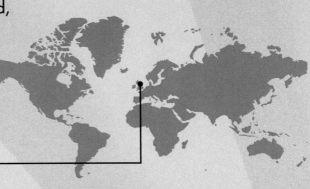

TOWERS AND TRUSSES

Three supporting towers resting on granite piers support the two truss girders. This formed the link spans connecting the north and south banks. An intricate network of steel trusses was then threaded through the length to carry two railway tracks down the middle. This design meant the end towers could be built on the solid ground of the riverbanks, with the middle tower resting on a natural island in the river. This avoided laying foundations in the unstable riverbed.

Once the piers were constructed and the steel towers added, the cantilever supports were built outward to form three massive diamond-shaped structures.

THE CANTILEVERED SOLUTION

In the 19th century, engineers had discovered that a longer span for a bridge could be achieved with a cantilevered design. This is achieved by anchoring the bridge platform at one end with further strengthening from staggered supports, making a structure like a giant diving board. If two of these spans were put together, the bridge could be really long and super strong. This was ideal for heavy rail bridges. It was this cantilevered design that Sir John Fowler chose for the Forth Bridge.

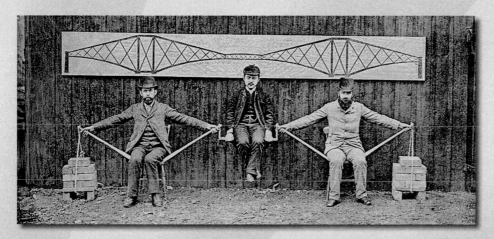

Forth Bridge engineers Sir John Fowler and Sir Benjamin Baker demonstrate how their bridge works with rope, bricks, and chairs. The weight of assistant Kaichi Watanabe (middle) is carried as compression through the lower beams, while the men's outstretched arms stop him from swaying.

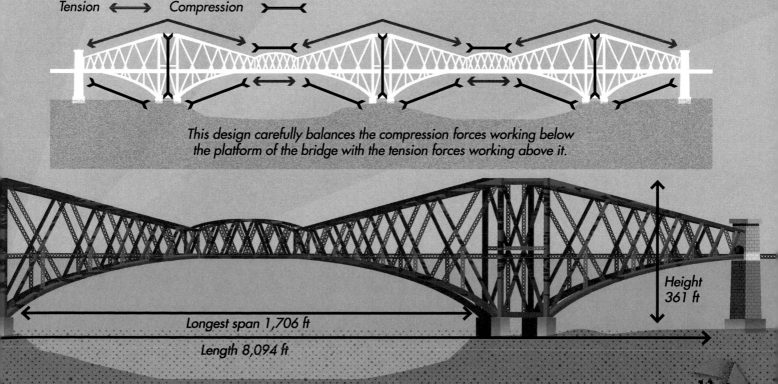

Tension ⟷   Compression ⟩⟩⟩

This design carefully balances the compression forces working below the platform of the bridge with the tension forces working above it.

Height 361 ft

Longest span 1,706 ft

Length 8,094 ft

VIZCAYA BRIDGE

Built in 1893, the Vizcaya Bridge crosses the Nervión River in Spain. It was the world's first transporter bridge, carrying traffic across the river on a suspended gondola. It's still in use today.

BUILDING BRIEF

Build a bridge to connect the towns of Portugalete and Gexto in the Biscay province of Spain. Make sure tall ships can sail underneath.

Designer: Alberto de Palacio

Engineer: Ferdinand Arnodin

Location: Biscay, Spain

The horizontal crossbeam is not welded to the towers. It rests on the corbels (supports) between the towers and is held in place by 70 steel suspension cables running from the main cable.

Height 200 ft

←⟶ Tension
⟩—⟨ Compression

DESIGN

This bridge features four 200-foot-high towers made from locally sourced iron. The towers were built on the dry land of each bank and feature a **lattice** pattern of beams. This makes them lightweight and allows wind to move through the structure.

The horizontal bridge platform and towers are held in place by suspension cables that are attached at the center of the towers. The cables are fastened to the ground on each bank. This design balances the forces of compression and tension throughout the bridge.

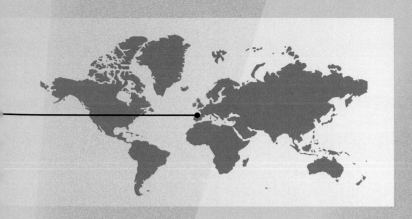

HANGING BRIDGE

The gondola dangles below the Vizcaya Bridge.

Locally, the bridge is called Puente Colgante, which is Spanish for "hanging bridge."

Unlike a traditional suspension bridge, the traffic does not move across the top but underneath it on a cable car, or gondola. The gondola can carry 200 people, six cars, and six bicycles on each 90-second crossing. Originally, a steam engine pulled the gondola, but this was changed to an electric system in 1901.

The gondola hangs on twisted steel cables.

Length 525 ft

TOWER BRIDGE

Tower Bridge is a major **landmark** in London, England. Opened in 1894, it's a combination of two bridge styles. It's a suspension bridge, featuring the famous towers, with a bascule bridge linking them. This swings upward to allow boats to continue up the river.

BUILDING BRIEF

Build a road and pedestrian bridge to cross the River Thames. It must allow access for sailing ships to pass under along the busy river.

Designer: Sir Horace Jones

Engineer: Sir John Wolfe Barry

Location: London, England, UK

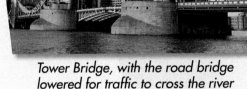

Tower Bridge, with the road bridge lowered for traffic to cross the river

WINNING DESIGN

In the late 1800s, **architects** competed to design a bridge to cross the River Thames. The winning design connected two bridge towers with a horizontal walkway. A bridge-lifting mechanism was hidden in the base of the towers. These are supported by two sets of double cables that stretch to smaller towers at each end of the bridge. The double cables are joined together by a criss-cross of bracings connecting to the bridge deck below.

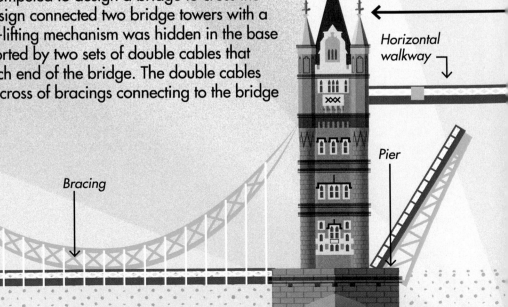

Horizontal walkway

Pier

Bracing

CONSTRUCTION

The towers are supported on two massive piers (the foundations) made from more than 770,000 tons of **concrete**. These were sunk into the riverbed during construction using caissons. It took four years just to do this! The towers and framework of the bridge were constructed from more than 12,000 tons of steel. Each tower has four upright steel pillars bolted to the granite piers.

BASCULE MECHANISM

Bascule comes from the French word for "seesaw." The deck of the bridge is made of two enormous **pivoting** seesaws. While about 100 ft of each bridge deck is visible, the other 60 ft is hidden within the bascule pit. This provides the **counterweight** to the rising part. Lead and iron add extra weight on the short end.

The rising parts of the bridge were originally powered by a hydraulic system. This system pumped water into an enclosed area, which raised the bridge. It was powered by steam engines on the south shore. The bridge could be opened in less than a minute. Today the steam and water system has been replaced by a mechanism powered by electricity and oil.

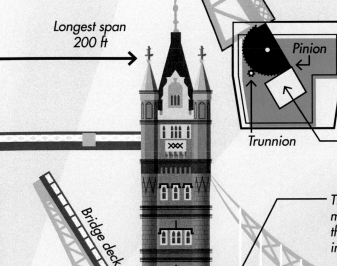

Bridge deck

Longest span 200 ft

Pinion

The bridge deck rests on trunnions, like the wheels that raise and lower a cannon. The decks are moved by pinions (or cog wheels), which engage with racks fixed to the edge of two steel cables connected to the outside girders.

Trunnion — Counterweight

Bridge deck

The pivots and machinery that move the bascule sections of the bridge are neatly hidden in the base of each tower.

800 ft

GOLDEN GATE BRIDGE

When it was completed in 1937, the Golden Gate Bridge in San Francisco, California, was the longest bridge in the world. At 8,981 ft, it was also a landmark in engineering. The graceful design and **iconic** orange paint have made it one of the most famous and most photographed bridges in the world.

BUILDING BRIEF

To build a bridge that spans nearly a mile of water. Must allow for changing temperatures, strong winds, sea currents, and for boats to pass underneath.

The engineers decided to build a suspension bridge. This type of bridge allows for the greatest distance to be covered with the least amount of materials and cost.

COMPRESSION AND TENSION

A suspension bridge relies on the **balanced forces** of compression and tension. The weight of the deck pulls on the vertical cables. This creates tension that transfers from the vertical cables into the main cables. The main cables are secured at anchorages at each end of the bridge. The tension is concentrated there. The towers hold the main cables up in the air and transfer the full weight of the bridge into the ground.

Compression is a force that pushes down.

Tension is a force that stretches.

Span between towers 4,200 ft

Engineers: Joseph B. Strauss and Charles A. Ellis

Location: San Francisco, California and Marin County, California, USA

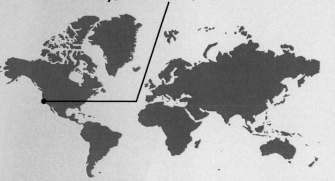

HOT AND COLD

San Francisco can get very hot and then much cooler. The engineers had to take into account the effect of changing weather on their materials.

As the temperature rises, the steel cables expand and lengthen, causing the deck to move closer to the water. As the temperature cools, the cables contract and shrink, and the bridge deck moves up.

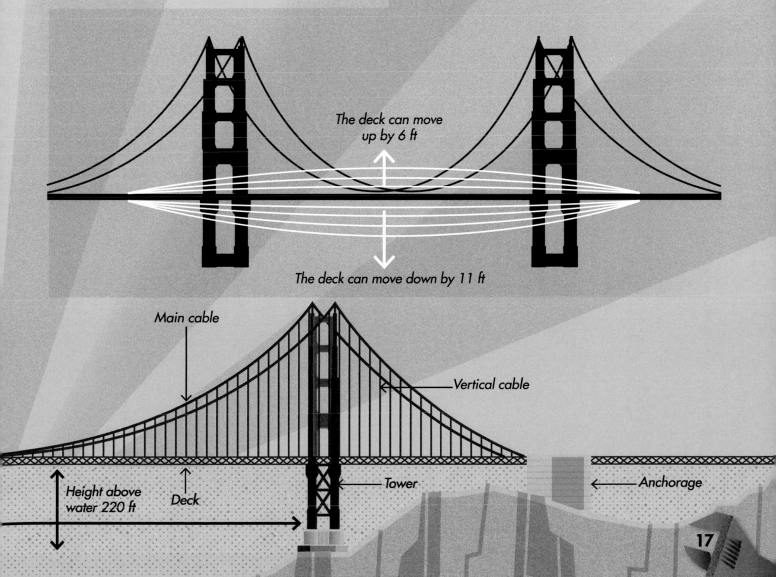

The deck can move up by 6 ft

The deck can move down by 11 ft

Main cable

Vertical cable

Height above water 220 ft

Deck

Tower

Anchorage

GOVERNOR ALBERT D. ROSELLINI BRIDGE
ALSO KNOWN AS EVERGREEN POINT FLOATING BRIDGE

One of the strangest solutions to bridge-building is a **pontoon** bridge that sits on the surface of the water. The Governor Albert D. Rosellini Bridge rests on Lake Washington, and it links Seattle to its eastern suburbs. Named the Evergreen Point Floating Bridge, it is the longest floating bridge in the world.

BUILDING BRIEF

Design a bridge to stretch across Lake Washington. The route needs to be curved, so a suspension bridge won't work. Plus, the lake is too deep for foundations.

Project by: Washington State Department of Transport

Location: Seattle, Washington

Total length
7,708 ft

The bridge deck sits on the floating pontoons.

OLD BRIDGE/NEW BRIDGE

The original bridge was built in 1963, but in 2016 it was replaced by a new version right beside it. The old bridge was showing signs of wear and needed to be made wider to deal with increased traffic.

The new bridge is the longest and widest floating bridge in the world. It stretches over the lake for an astonishing 7,708 ft, with a midpoint width of 115 ft. Compared to the old bridge, it has an extra lane in each direction, plus a path for pedestrians and cyclists.

PONTOONS

Pontoons are floating concrete blocks on which the bridge sits. A total of 77 pontoons stretch across the lake. These have hollow partitioned centers that allow them to float and keep the bridge stable.

The bridge deck floats on Lake Washington.

Pontoon

Water level

ANCHORS

There are three different types of anchors used on the pontoons:

The pontoons are secured to the bottom of the lake by 58 anchors. The anchor points are located at various depths, and the chains pull at different angles, creating an enormous backbone for the bridge deck. The anchors secure the pontoons to stop the bridge from floating away but also use tension forces to keep it all aligned.

Gravity anchors are used in solid soils closer to the shore. These are 40 ft x 40 ft x 24 ft concrete boxes filled with rocks.

Drilled shaft anchors are concrete cylinders hidden in the ground near the shore.

Fluke anchors are used in softer soils, deep in the lakebed.

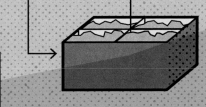

AKASHI-KAIKYŌ BRIDGE

Although the Akashi-Kaikyō Bridge has been standing since 1998, it is still the longest, tallest, and most expensive suspension bridge in the world. It stretches an incredible 12,831 ft across the Akashi Strait, linking mainland Japan with Awaji Island.

BUILDING BRIEF

Construct a safe bridge from Kobe to the island of Awaji to replace ferry crossings. It has to cover a vast distance and be strong enough to withstand hurricanes, **tsunamis**, strong currents, and earthquakes.

Designer: Satoshi Kashima

Location: Awaji Island and Kobe, Japan

COLOSSAL FOUNDATIONS

The two gigantic towers have concrete foundations that were constructed by sinking molds to the seabed. These molds were flooded with seawater, and then special concrete was added that could be submerged before setting. The foundations go down almost 200 ft, the depth of a 20-story building. Another 385,000 tons of concrete were used at each end of the bridge to make the cable anchor blocks.

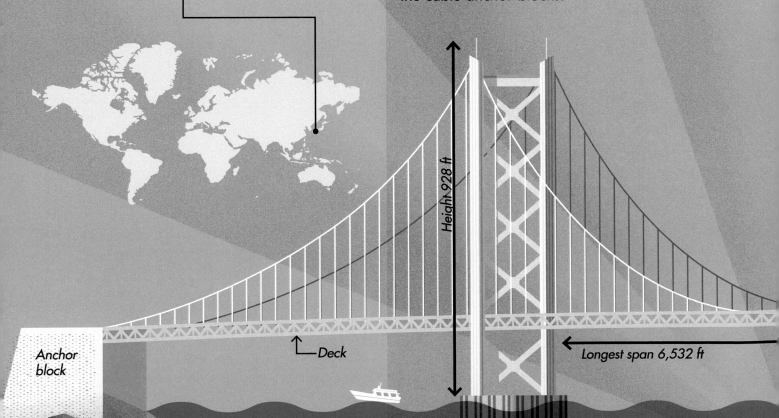

Anchor block

Deck

Height 928 ft

Longest span 6,532 ft

TUNED MASS DAMPER TOWERS

In the towers, engineers added 20 tuned mass dampers, which are like large weighted **pendulums**. These sway in the opposite direction to the bridge to help control and minimize movement during strong winds.

During construction, the main supporting towers had been finished when the Great Hanshin Earthquake struck in 1995. The towers held strong, but the earthquake had moved them farther apart. The span between the towers had to be increased by more than 3 feet.

TRIANGULAR STRENGTH

The bridge is so long that the deck needs to be very strong to stop it from twisting in the wind. The deck is a very stiff lattice of steel girders called a truss. The triangular lattice adds strength but also allows the winds to whistle through. The bridge can handle wind speeds as high as 180 miles per hour!

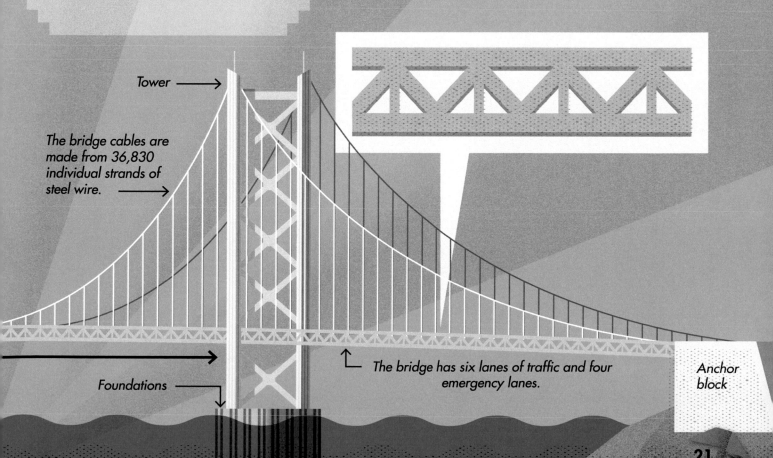

Tower ⟶

The bridge cables are made from 36,830 individual strands of steel wire. ⟶

Foundations ⟶

↑ *The bridge has six lanes of traffic and four emergency lanes.*

Anchor block

JUSCELINO KUBITSCHEK BRIDGE

The architect of the Juscelino Kubitschek Bridge wanted to make it look like a stone skipping the water. So while the components are strong and functional, it has a dynamic feel. Opened in 2002, it carries road, cycle, and pedestrian traffic across Lake Paranoá in Brasília, Brazil.

The design of the bridge helps to distribute the weight along the span. The load is shared between the under deck supports, the arches that criss-cross over the main bridge, and the foundations. The arches support the main deck with downward cables connected to both sides of the roadway. The arches and cables are made from steel, while the supports and deck are concrete.

BUILDING BRIEF

Win the competition to design and build a bridge to join new areas of the city across Lake Paranoá in central Brasília and be a focal point for Brazil's capital city.

Architect: Alexandre Chan

Engineer: Mário Vila Verde

Location: Brasília, Brazil

ARCH SUPPORTS

All three arches had to be built and positioned at the same time to keep the load on the bridge balanced. The base of each arch is concrete as it enters the water, but it changes to steel as it curves overhead.

The arches were built in sections that were then floated, lifted, and welded into place. Welding on the steel arch was done at night because welding would not have been so successful in the high temperatures of the daytime.

In 2003, the bridge won the ABCEM Award for best steel construction. It was recognized for "showing harmony with the environment, **aesthetic** merit, and successful community participation."

the impressive Juscelino Kubitschek Bridge reflected in Lake Paranoá, Brazil

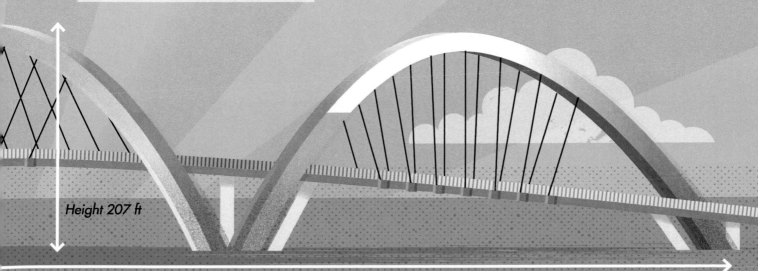

Height 207 ft

Length 3,937 ft

MILLAU VIADUCT

Completed in 2004, the Millau Viaduct elegantly crosses the River Tarn in the south of France. It is the tallest bridge in the world, with support towers reaching 1,125 ft in height. The structure was designed to look light and slender.

CABLE PROTECTION

The Millau Viaduct is a cable-stayed bridge that features seven supporting towers intersected by the road deck. From the top of the towers, 11 pairs of stays project down and fan out along the middle of the deck, holding it in place. Each stay is made from between 55 and 91 steel cables. Each cable is made from seven strands of steel wire. Each strand is **galvanized** to protect it from corrosion, coated with petroleum wax, and finally wrapped in a polythene cover.

BUILDING BRIEF

Design and build a bridge to complete a roadway linking Paris to the Mediterranean coast and Spain, crossing the gorge of the River Tarn between two high **plateaus.**

Architect: Norman Foster

Engineer: Michel Virlogeux

Location: Millau, France

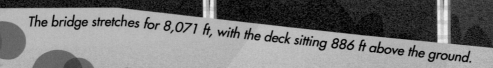

The bridge stretches for 8,071 ft, with the deck sitting 886 ft above the ground.

COLUMNS

The towering columns that extend from the ground to the deck were made of concrete shaped in molds called formwork. They had to be made in stages. When one section of the concrete pillar was set, the mold was moved up and the next load of concrete was poured in. Slowly the towers grew taller.

The support pylons that hold the cables are made from steel and are an integral part of the bridge deck. These pylon and deck pieces were built on land and then pushed into place along temporary columns and supports.

"We wanted the piers to look as if they had barely alighted on the landscape, light and delicate—like butterflies' legs."

Norman Foster, architect

DECK

The deck is made up of 173 welded steel pieces topped with a special **bitumen** road surface. The surface needed to be good for motorway driving—long-lasting and nonslip—while being flexible to allow for changes in the steel deck below. It took two years to find the right mixture.

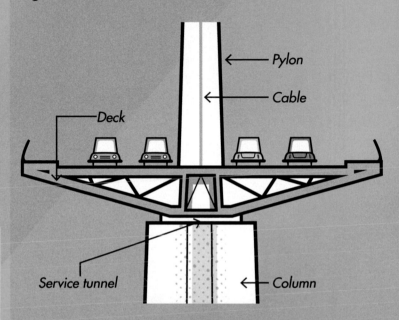

This cross section shows the streamlined shape of the deck support, the four lanes for traffic, and the service tunnel.

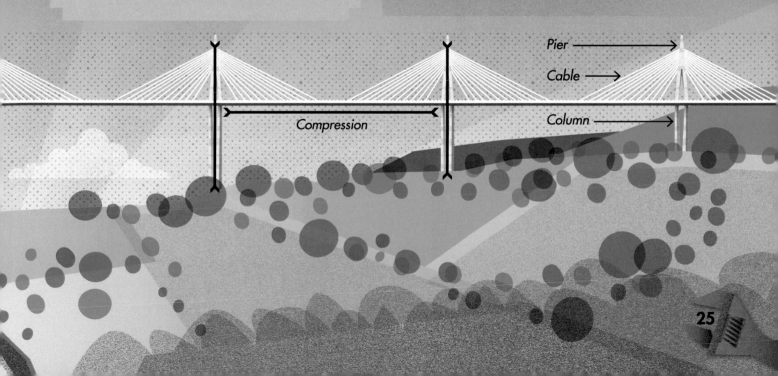

25

THE HELIX

The **Helix** in Singapore is a bridge that crosses Marina Bay. Opened in 2010, it was inspired by the geometric, twisting shape of a **DNA** molecule. It's a shimmering display of glass and steel that adds a feeling of movement to the structure.

BUILDING BRIEF

Design and build a landmark pedestrian bridge. It should curve across the harbor and provide shelter from the tropical rain and sun.

Engineers: Arup

Architects: Cox Architecture with Architects 61

Location: Marina Bay, Singapore

COMPUTER MODELING

The design for the bridge was tested on 3D computer software. This enabled the engineers to test the difficult helix shapes they wanted to use, specify the shape and fit of each steel piece, and accurately plan the amount of materials needed. The software also allowed them to test **stress** and vibrations from pedestrians and model how the bridge would hold up if damage occurred.

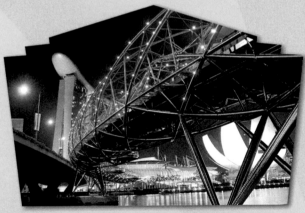

Lit up by LEDs, the bridge looks magical at night.

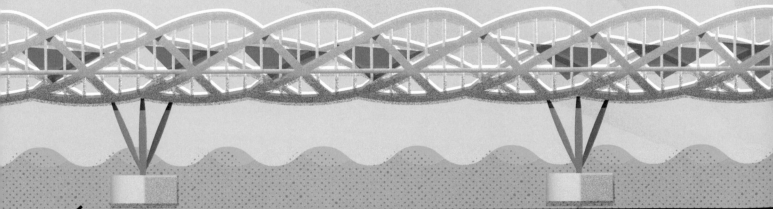

Length 919 ft

26

TUBULAR TRUSS

The bridge is constructed from tubular steel and features two winding helix shapes. The inner helix has a glass ceiling in places, which provides shelter for pedestrians when the weather gets too hot or rainy. The helix shapes are held in place by a criss-cross of trusses, which make a super-strong latticework frame.

TRIPOD SUPPORTS

The whole bridge rests on upside-down **tripod**-shaped tubular supports. Each of the supporting steel columns is filled with concrete and joined to the foundations. The spans in between these supports are up to 213 ft long.

"The Helix is truly an engineering marvel. While the structure is incredibly delicate and intricate, it's been engineered to support more than 10,000 people at a time. The Helix is the first example of this structural solution applied to a bridge—there is nothing else like it."
Dr. See Lin Ming,
Arup Project Leader

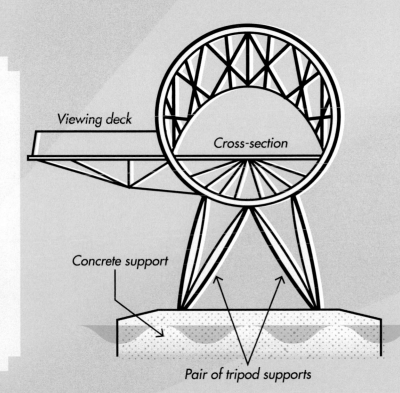

Viewing deck

Cross-section

Concrete support

Pair of tripod supports

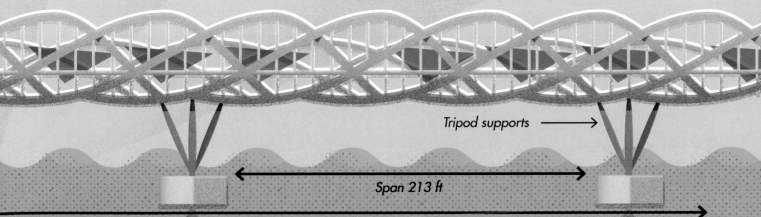

Tripod supports →

Span 213 ft

FASCINATING FACTS

Bridges come in many wonderful shapes and sizes. Here are some fascinating facts about awesome bridges from around the world.

The Gateshead Millennium Bridge is a pedestrian and cycle bridge over the River Tyne in the UK. The whole structure tips up with the help of water power, allowing boats to pass underneath. It's like a gigantic winking eyelid.

The double-decker Umshiang Living Root Bridge is located in Cherrapunjee, in northeastern India. It was made by training tree roots to cross the river and then attach and grow there. It can take 15 years to grow a usable bridge.

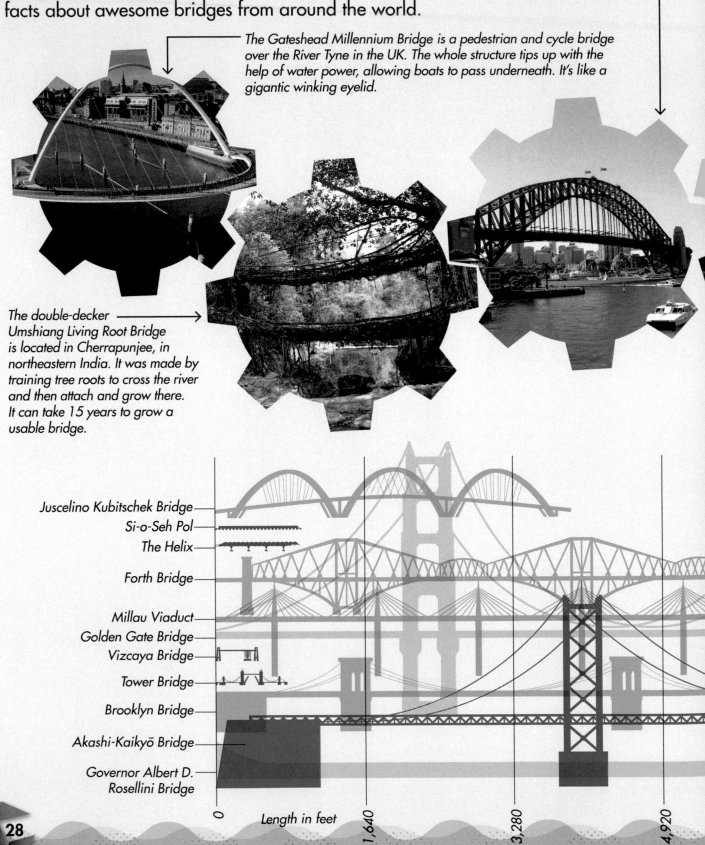

Juscelino Kubitschek Bridge
Si-o-Seh Pol
The Helix
Forth Bridge
Millau Viaduct
Golden Gate Bridge
Vizcaya Bridge
Tower Bridge
Brooklyn Bridge
Akashi-Kaikyō Bridge
Governor Albert D. Rosellini Bridge

0   Length in feet   1,640   3,280   4,920

The Sydney Harbor Bridge in Australia opened in 1932 and is nicknamed "The Coathanger" because of its arched metal shape. It's made from 58,200 tons of steel and six million **rivets**.

At 24 miles long, the Lake Pontchartrain Causeway in Louisiana is the world's longest bridge that's continuously over water. For 8 miles, land is not visible in either direction, making for a scary drive.

The Henderson Waves Bridge is the highest pedestrian bridge in Singapore at 118 ft. Made from steel strips that rise above and fall below the bridge deck, it looks like waves flowing through the treetops.

Ponte Vecchio has spanned the River Arno in Florence, Italy, since 1345. It has a raised corridor built above the bridge deck that allowed Cosimo I de Medici—the Duke of Florence—to cross without being bothered by locals. Today, this corridor is part of the Uffizi Gallery.

6,560   8,200   9,840   11,480   13,120

READ MORE

Cornille, Didier. *Bridges: An Introduction to Ten Great Bridges and Their Designers.* Who Built That? New York: Princeton Architectural Press, 2016.

Hoena, Blake. *Building the Golden Gate Bridge: An Interactive Engineering Adventure.* Engineering Marvels. Mankato, Minn.: Capstone Press, 2015.

Mattern, Joanne. *Bridges. Engineering Wonders.* Vero Beach, Fla.: Rourke Educational Media, 2015.

INTERNET SITES

FactHound offers a safe, fun way to find Internet sites related to this book. All of the sites on FactHound have been researched by our staff.

Here's all you do:

Visit www.facthound.com

Type in this code: 9781543513349

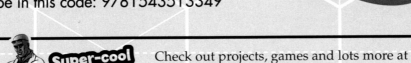

Check out projects, games and lots more at
www.capstonekids.com

GLOSSARY

abutment something against which another thing rests its weight or pushes with force

aesthetic having to do with art and beauty or with things that are beautiful

anchor to fasten to a firm foundation; an anchorage is the place where something is secured

architect a person who designs buildings, bridges, and other construction projects

balanced forces when two forces acting on an object are equal and act in opposite directions to keep an object steady and still

bedrock the solid layer of rock under the soil, clay, or sand

bitumen an oily, black tar substance used for surfacing roads and roofs

caisson a tube or box in which people and machines can work under water; caissons are later filled with concrete and used to support bridges and buildings

cantilevers beams or structures that stick out from piers toward each other and when joined form a span in a bridge

compression the stress on a structure from a force pushing or pressing against it

concrete a building material made from a mixture of sand, gravel, cement, and water

counterweight a weight that balances a load

deck a floor or platform; a bridge deck is the road vehicles travel on

designer a person who thinks up ideas and draws out plans for new products

DNA material in cells that gives people their individual characteristics; DNA stands for deoxyribonucleic acid

earthenware pottery made from baked clay

engineer someone who designs and builds roads, machines, vehicles, bridges, or other structures

force any action, such as pushing or pulling, that changes the movement of an object

foundation the base or solid structure on which a building is built

galvanize to coat steel or iron with zinc to keep it from rusting

helix something spiral in form

iconic an object or person that is famous, popular, and admired

iron a hard metal used in buildings; cast iron is made from an alloy of iron, carbon, and silicon

landmark an object that stands out as important, such as a big tree or a building

lattice a pattern formed by strips of material that cross each other diagonally

limestone a hard white or gray stone, often used as a building material

live load the total force or weight that a structure is designed to withstand or hold

parapet a low wall or railing on the edge of a platform, roof, or bridge

pendulum something that hangs from a fixed point so it swings freely under the force of gravity

pivot a point on which something turns or balances

plateau an area of flat land that is higher than the surrounding area

pontoon a floating support for a bridge or other structure

rivet a metal bolt or pin used to hold metal objects together

shear to push in one direction from the top and the opposite direction from the bottom

silt small particles of soil that settle at the bottom of a river, lake, or ocean

steel a strong, hard metal formed from iron, carbon, and other materials

stress the physical pressure, pull, or other force on an object

torsion to twist one end of an object away from the other end

tripod a three-legged stand

truss a framework of metal or wooden beams used to support objects, such as bridges, walls, or roofs

tsunami a very large, destructive wave caused by an underwater earthquake or volcano

weld to join two pieces of metal together by heating them until they melt

INDEX